Maps in History

Maps in History

Walter Oleksy

Watts LIBRARY™

Franklin Watts
A Division of Scholastic Inc.
New York • Toronto • London • Auckland • Sydney
Mexico City • New Delhi • Hong Kong
Danbury, Connecticut

To Justin and Kaitlyn Ohde

Note to readers: Definitions for words in **bold** can be found in the Glossary at the back of this book.

Photographs © 2002: AKG London/Bibliotheque Nationale, Paris: 14; Art Resource, NY: 34 (Gilder Lehrman Collection, Pierpont Morgan Library, photo by Joseph Zehavi), 2, 16, 26 (Giraudon), 22 (Scala), 21 (Uffizi Gallery, Firenze), 5 left, 28; Beinecke Rare Book and Manuscript Library, Yale University: 24; Bridgeman Art Library International Ltd., London/New York: 6, 27 (British Museum, London, UK), 11 (Louvre, Paris, France), 40, 42 (Private Collection); Christie's Images: 20; Corbis Images: 37; Hulton Archive/Liaison/Getty Images: 13; North Wind Picture Archives: 5 right, 9, 32, 38; Photo Researchers, NY/George & Judy Manna: 17; Photri Inc.: 45, 47, 48; Stone/Getty Images/David Young-Wolff: 49; Superstock, Inc.: 18 (Christie's Images), 36 (David David Gallery, Philadelphia), cover.

The photograph on the cover shows a close-up of a world map by John Speed made in 1626. The photograph opposite the title page shows a map of Europe by Antonio Varese.

Library of Congress Cataloging-in-Publication Data

Oleksy, Walter G., 1930–
    Maps in history / by Walter Oleksy
        p. cm. — (Watts library)
    Includes bibliographical references and index.
    ISBN 0-531-12028-7 (lib. bdg.)   0-531-16633-3 (pbk.)
    1. Cartography—History—Juvenile literature. [1. Cartography—History. 2. Maps] I. Title. II. Series.
GA105.6 .O38 2001
526—dc21
                                                                                                2001017561

Contents

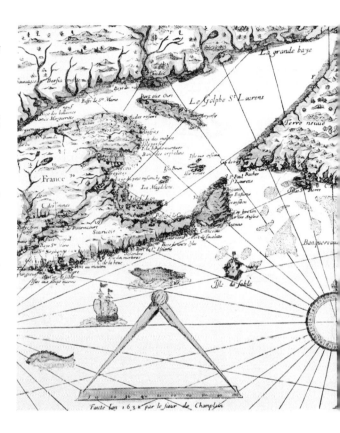

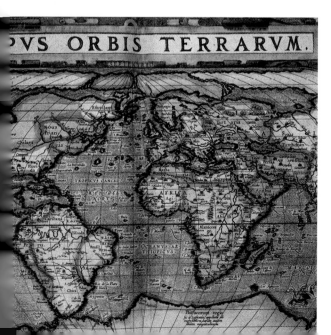

This clay tablet is a Babylonian map that dates back to the 500s B.C.

Chapter One

Early Maps and Mapmaking

The first **maps** were made on animal skins and cave walls by cave dwellers. They defined the **boundaries** of tribes and recorded routes to hunting grounds. The cave dwellers also recorded where their enemies lived and hunted.

Clay maps dating back to 2300 B.C. have been found in Babylonia, now part of Iraq. The best-known clay map is the

Akkadian map, often described as the oldest map in the world. Another Babylonian clay tablet made in about 500 B.C. shows settlements, waterways, and mountains. Babylonians were the first to develop the system of dividing a circle into 360 degrees. This later became important in mapmaking, allowing people to measure **latitude** and **longitude**.

Other ancient civilizations were active in mapmaking. Egyptians began making maps before 1000 B.C. They had to re-map property boundaries every year after the Nile River flooded its banks. The ancient Greeks used geometry and surveyed the land, which means to measure the angles, distances, and heights to determine the location and boundaries of places. This information enabled them to develop map **projections**—ways of showing the curved surface of the Earth on a flat piece of paper.

Polynesian Explorers

Mapmakers throughout history have owed a great deal to seagoing **explorers**. They discovered new islands, countries, and continents. The Polynesians were among the earliest and most adventuresome explorers. They sailed to distant lands and brought back information used in mapmaking.

Polynesians originally lived on the islands of Papua New Guinea. By 1000 B.C., however, their islands became too crowded and they set sail in small canoes with no **compass** or **sea charts** to find new land to settle on. Polynesian explorers made stick maps from bamboo sticks and shells to record their voyages. The sticks depicted **currents** and waves, and the shells represented islands.

Over the next two thousand years, Polynesian sailors discovered islands in the Pacific Ocean from New Zealand to Hawaii, which are known today as the Polynesian Islands. The sailors found them by following the Sun and stars, noting changes in winds and ocean currents, often desperately looking for birds that might lead them to land. Their perilous voyages helped map the great central heart of the Pacific Ocean.

Polynesians explored the Pacific Ocean in sea canoes.

Early Mapmakers

The first mapmakers based their maps on information about distant lands brought back by explorers. One of the earliest explorers who returned with valuable information for mapmakers was Hanno, a sea captain from Carthage in North Africa. He led a fleet of sixty boats each manned by fifty oarsmen, although the boats also had sails.

Hanno sailed his fleet through the Strait of Gibraltar into the Atlantic Ocean in 470 B.C. He and his crew explored the northwest coast of Africa and opened trade with people living there. Upon his return, Hanno told tales of his travels, including his encounters with huge hairy creatures called gorillas. These stories helped mapmakers draw the first maps of parts of Africa.

Hanno's adventures became useful to future **cartographers** such as Claudius Ptolemaeus, a Greek mathematician and astronomer. Known as Ptolemy, he drew maps in Alexandria, Egypt, about A.D. 150. He published his own knowledge of

The Earth's Circumference

The first measurement of the **circumference** of the Earth was made in 240 B.C. by a Greek mathematician, Eratosthenes of Alexandria. He did this by recording the angle of a shadow cast by a stick at Alexandria on the day of the summer solstice, when there was no shadow at Aswan, about 500 miles (800 km) to the south. He then divided the figure —7.5 degrees—into 360 degrees. Considered among the great achievements of Greek science, it also convinced many people that the Earth was indeed a sphere.

Along with Geography, *Ptolemy published many other works, such as* Almagest, *a 13-volume set on astronomy.*

mapmaking and that of others from earlier times in an eight-volume set of books entitled *Geography*. The books told how to make map projections and listed about eight thousand places in the then-known world, including their longitude and latitude.

Map Grids

A grid is a network or pattern of equally spaced vertical and horizontal lines, which are all **perpendicular** to each other. The lines form squares that show the location of places on a map.

Geography remained the most authoritative reference on maps for almost one thousand years.

At about the same time as Ptolemy, Chang Heng, a Chinese astronomer, developed perhaps the first geographic **grid** system for maps. In mapmaking, a grid is a network of **horizontal** and **vertical** lines that allows you to find places on a map by means of a system of coordinates. Hand-drawn silk maps with grids helped the Chinese locate places in the late 200s B.C.

Mapping the Silk Road

Not all explorers opened up new worlds by sailing to distant lands. Many others whose journeys helped map remote areas traveled by land. One such explorer was Zhang Qian, a young man who worked in the palace of the emperor of China in 138 B.C.

The emperor needed someone to travel west through enemy territory, to ask the Scythian tribes of central Asia to help fight their common enemy, the Huns. Zhang Qian volunteered to lead the expedition. He set out from the emperor's palace at Xi'am with one hundred men and as many horses and camels.

Crossing high snowy mountains, they reached the land of the Huns, but were captured. After ten years in captivity, Zhang Qian and a few of his companions managed to escape. They finally reached the Scythians, but were unable to persuade them to help fight the Huns.

Zhang Qian's journey to China was not a failure, however. On his way, he learned of the riches of Rome and India. He returned to China urging trade with the lands to the west. This led to what became known as the Silk Road, one of the most famous trade routes of all time. More than just a single road, the Silk Road became the name for all the trading routes that brought silk from China into Europe from about 100 B.C. into the A.D. 1300s.

This illustration shows the explorer Marco Polo traveling on the Silk Road.

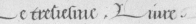

This page from a French book shows a circular, or T-O, map, which was a common type of map in the Middle Ages.

Cy commece le xiij liure qparle de leaue et de ses ptics...

Re ceuptes les ptiees du feu et de lair. il est temps que nous dises maintenant de leaue et de ses euures entant côme il en ptient a ceste petite euure. Leaue est ainsi appellee

Le premier chapitre parle de leaue en general ptire quelle est egalle et vnie. car elle ne cesse onques desoy mouuoir tant qlle est toute esgalle par dessus sicôme dit ysidore. ou xiij. liure des ethmologies. Leaue selon côstantin est vng element froit et moite subtil et delie et der au ie

Chapter Two

Maps in the Middle Ages

Most maps of the early Middle Ages (A.D. 400 to about the 1300s) were circular maps showing Jerusalem as the center of the world, to satisfy Christian **theologians**, those who study religion. Circular maps were called T-O maps. A circle, or the O, was divided into three parts of the enclosed T. These maps were only partly geographical in nature, since they depicted theological and philosophical beliefs of the time. Early world maps had east at the top and north to the left.

The most important advancements in mapmaking during the Middle Ages took place in the Arab world and in China. Ptolemy's *Geography*, translated into Arabic in the 800s, helped Arab mapmakers calculate latitude and longitude for their nation's soldiers and traders. The Arabian cartographer al-Idrisi drew a rectangular world map on seventy sheets of paper that compiled geographic information from travelers in the mid-1100s. At that same time, an unknown Chinese mapmaker made a carved stone map of China that included its coastline and many rivers, villages, and towns.

Christian crusades into the Holy Land—present-day Israel, Jordan, and Egypt—during this time contributed to mapmaking knowledge in the vast eastern regions. The

This photograph shows a map of South India made by al-Idrisi.

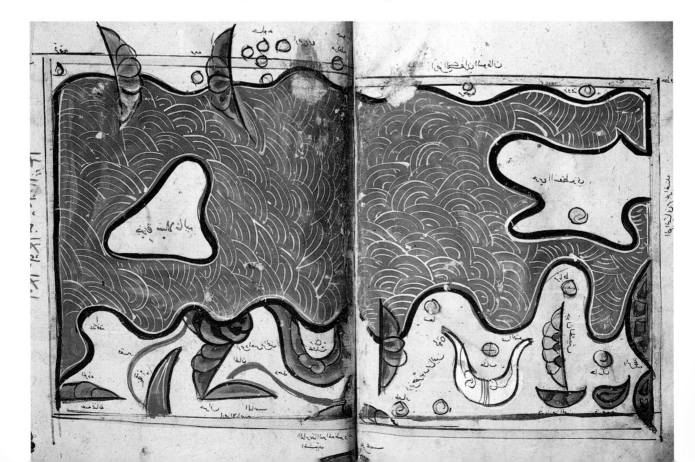

crusades were a series of wars undertaken by European Christians during the Middle Ages. Their purpose was to win back the Holy Land and other regions from the Muslims.

One crusader-explorer was Guillaume of Rubruqiuis of Flanders. In 1253, he was sent by King Louis IX of France to assist in converting the Tartar, or Tatar, people to Christianity in what is now Mongolia. While he had little success in completing his mission, Guillaume told the king about the area's important geographical features, such as the Don and Volga Rivers. He also observed that the Caspian Sea was actually a lake.

The Compass

A compass is an instrument used in **navigation** to show direction. It contains a freely suspended magnetic needle that always points to magnetic north. Historians do not know how, when, or where the compass was invented. The first reference of the compass in European literature dates from the 1100s.

Portolan Charts

Near the end of the Middle Ages, in the late 1200s and early 1300s, Italian sea captains began making navigational maps called **portolan charts**. The charts showed the shorelines of the Mediterranean and Black Seas with what, even today, is considered remarkable accuracy. Portolan charts noted inlets and bays, mountains, rivers, and other landmarks that could be used to steer ships. Lines drawn across each chart also helped sailors determine compass directions.

The red lines on this map were used to chart courses across the waters.

One of the great early users of portolan charts was Henry the Navigator, a Portuguese prince with a passion for exploration. His voyages in the early 1400s enabled him to gather knowledge of the ocean and inland regions of West and North Africa. This information, recorded on maps that were highly treasured and kept secret from foreign powers, allowed Portugal to build a major colonial empire in the 1500s.

Printing Maps

While the earliest-known printed map appeared in a Chinese encyclopedia in about 1155, it would be more than three hundred years before printed maps were seen in Europe. Many early maps in the Western world were simple woodcut reproductions and were not very accurate. Until the late Middle Ages, European cartographers laboriously copied maps and portolan charts by hand. It was a time-consuming process that required great patience and artistic skills.

It took one invention to revolutionize mapmaking in Europe. In 1436 or 1437, Johannes Gutenberg, a German printer, became the first European to print with movable type cast in molds. His first great printed work was the Bible, which had previously been copied by hand. He then printed many copies of maps and charts in a much shorter time than it took others to hand-draw them. The invention of the printing press also made maps and charts more widely available.

The World: Flat or Round?

As late as the 1400s, some uneducated people still believed the Earth was flat, despite the existence of globes that made the world look round. People feared a ship could sail far into the ocean, and then fall off the face of the Earth. The historic voyage of Portuguese navigator Ferdinand Magellan proved that the world was, indeed, round.

Magellan set sail from Spain in 1519 with five ships and 280 men. After circumnavigating, or going around, the world from west to east, only one ship returned home—three years later—with eighteen survivors on board. Magellan himself did not survive the historic voyage. He was killed in a dispute between rival native peoples in the Philippines on April 27, 1521.

Globes

Globes of the world, three-dimensional sphere or round maps, date back centuries. A forerunner of globes was a cylinder on which a Greek geographer, Anaximander of Miletus, drew a map in about 550 B.C. He believed that the world was a cylinder, with the habitable world as a disk at the top.

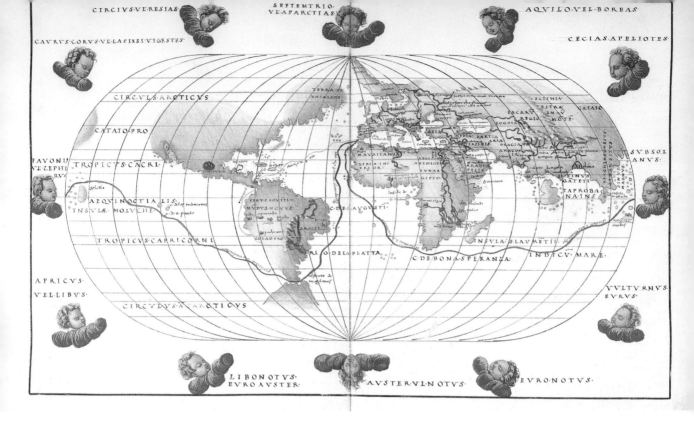

The map shows a world map with various Latin labels including CIRCIVS VERESIAS, SEPTEMTRIO VEL APARCTIAS, AQVILO VEL BOREAS, CAVRVS CORVS VELA PIXSI VIGESTES, CECIAS APELIOTES, CIRCVLVS ARCTICVS, TERRA DE BACALAOS, SCITHIA, CATATO PRO, FAVONV VEL ZEPHI RVS, TROPICVS CNCRI, AEQVINOCTIALIS, INSVLE MOLVCHE, MVDVS NOVVS, BRAZILL, TROPICVS CAPRICORNI, AFRICVS VELLIBVS, CIRCVLVS ATARCTICVS, MAVRITANIA, LIBIA INFERIOR, DVBAE, GIFFO, ETHIOPIA, C DE S AVGVSTI, RIO DELA PLATTA, C DE BONA SPERANZA, INSVLA S LAVRETII, INDICV MARE, TAPROBANA INS, SVBSOLANVS, VVLTVRNVS EVRVS, LIBONOTVS EVROAVSTER, AVSTER VEL NOTVS, EVRONOTVS

The thick blue line shows Magellan's journey around the world.

After Magellan's voyage around the world proved the Earth was not flat, mapmakers struggled to create maps showing the spherical Earth on a flat piece of paper. Navigators needed a flat map to plot courses more easily. They could only chart their courses on paper, not on cumbersome globes. Flat maps were drawn by means of map projection. A map projection transfers the round surface of the globe onto a flat surface such as paper.

In 1492, a German navigator and astronomer, Martin Behaim, created the first globe in the modern Western world. However, the terrestrial globe showed the world as European navigators knew it before Christopher Columbus's voyage, so it did not include North or South America. Also, repeating

Ptolemy's inaccuracy, the globe showed the Atlantic Ocean as being much smaller than it actually is.

North and South America were not included on maps and globes until the early 1500s. The first time the word *America* appeared on a map was in 1507, on a map made by German cartographer Martin Waldseemüller. He named the new continent after an Italian navigator, Amerigo Vespucci. His America also did not refer to North America, but referred only to the South American continent.

Amerigo Vespucci

Amerigo Vespucci, the Italian navigator for whom America was named, supervised and updated Spain's official maps and charts. He sailed from Spain to the West Indies in 1499, discovering and exploring the source of the Amazon River. Then he sailed along the northern coast of South America, becoming the first to recognize it as a new continent and not part of Asia.

Vespucci also made a name for himself in navigation history by devising a system that computed nearly exact longitude. Using ancient instruments he determined the Earth's equatorial circumference at only 50 miles (80 km) less than what it actually is.

He became a high-ranking pilot major, but many scholars of the time did not believe his successes. Denied fame and fortune, he died of malaria, an illness he contracted on his voyages.

This is a map of the world made in Italy during the Renaissance.

Chapter Three

Maps in the Renaissance

Great advances were made in mapmaking during the Renaissance (the 1400s to 1500s). The period was also known as the Age of Discovery because so many new discoveries were made in science and other fields of learning. Ptolemy's maps of the world were rediscovered in Europe in the 1400s when *Geography* was translated into Latin. This set the stage for bold new sea explorations that led to the discoveries of far distant parts of the world.

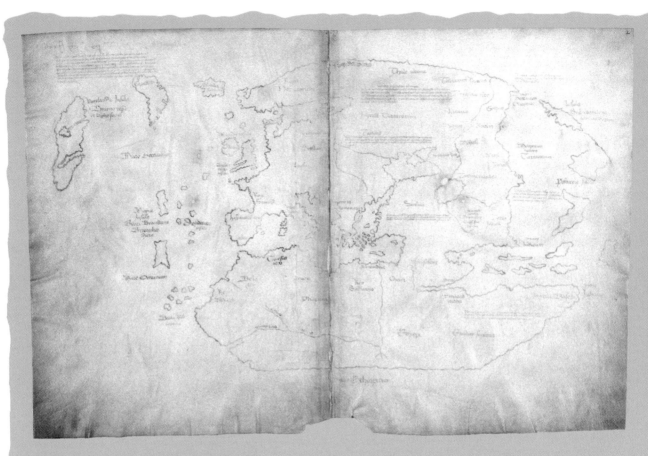

The Great Mystery Map

For centuries, historians agreed that Christopher Columbus sailed from Spain on August 3, 1492, and was the first to reach the land that became known as America. He arrived on an island near Cuba, naming it San Salvador, on October 12. But in 1965, researchers at Yale University stunned the world by reporting the discovery of a map dated before 1440 that showed the eastern coast of North America. The map became known as the Vinland Map because it showed an island labeled *Vinlanda Insula*, which means Island of Vinland. Vikings, sea-faring warriors from Scandinavia, were known to have sailed to Greenland—also known as Vinland because of the dense vines that grew there—located far north in the Atlantic Ocean, as early as A.D. 985.

In 1974, however, researchers studying the Vinland Map declared it to be a forgery. Then, after much study and testing, a panel of map experts concluded the map is authentic in 1996. Others, however, remain unconvinced, which makes the Vinland Map perhaps the most controversial map in history.

However, sea captains, such as Christopher Columbus, were to discover that Ptolemy was not as accurate as they had hoped. His estimate of the Earth's circumference was about one-third smaller than it actually is. The Earth's circumference at the equator is 24,902.4 miles (40,076.5 km). Following a map patterned after Ptolemy's, Columbus sailed in search of a western passage to the Orient. Instead, he wound up in the Americas.

Ptolemy Got It Wrong

For centuries, cartographers and explorers relied on Ptolemy's ancient map. It was drawn more than 1,400 years ago, and it was far from correct in many ways. But that was only to be expected, since no one had actually seen many of the eight thousand distant lands he drew on his map.

According to Ptolemy, Africa joined a large land called the Unknown Continent. However, in 1488, a Portuguese sailor, Bartolomeu Dias, proved Africa had a southern border. He learned this by sailing to its southern tip around what became known as the Cape of Good Hope. Dias called it the Cape of Storms, and sailed far enough around it to see that the land continued from there.

Ptolemy also confused Asia with North America. On his map, Asia appeared where North America actually lies. And the map showed neither North nor South America. Those continents would not be discovered until centuries after Ptolemy.

Ptolemy was also wrong about the size of the Earth. The

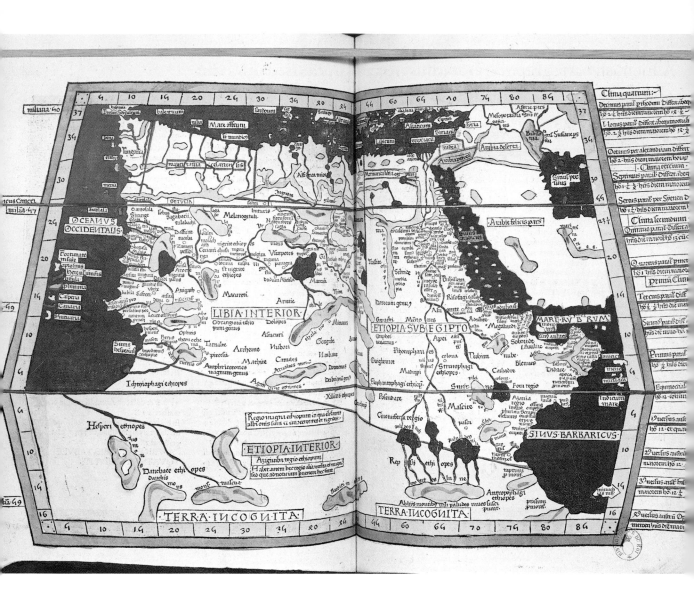

Ptolemy's work was used as the basis for maps for centuries. This map of Africa was made in 1486.

world is one-third larger than shown on his map. This misled navigators such as Magellan. Following the map, he believed his ship could sail around the tip of South America and enter the Pacific Ocean in just a few days. The distances were far greater and the voyage took more than three months, during which time most of his crew starved.

Map Projections

A Flemish cartographer, Gerardus Mercator, devised a system of map projection that allowed mapmakers to convert information from a round globe onto a flat surface. Maps are made from different viewpoints called projections. In map terms, a projection is any arrangement of **meridians** and **parallels** of the curving surface of the round Earth drawn on a flat paper surface.

Mercator made this map of Europe around 1554.

27

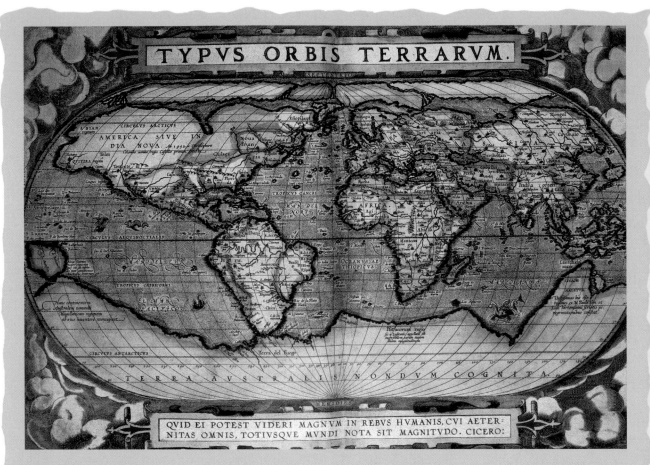

The First Atlas

The first modern world **atlas**—a collection of maps in one book—was the *Theatrum Orbis Terrarum*, produced in 1570 by the Flemish mapmaker, Abraham Ortelius. It contained seventy maps he compiled in part from eighty-seven cartographers. A 1587 edition contained 103 maps. He became geographer to Phillip II of Spain.

The Mercator projection map in which the surface of the Earth is shown as a flat rectangle was published in 1569. It was a great help in navigation because it enabled a path to be determined in any direction as a straight line. A sailor could draw a line from point A to point B and sail at that constant compass setting. However, that line, known as a Rhumb line, may not be the shortest distance between the two points.

The Age of Enlightenment

The intellectual developments of the Renaissance were followed by a period of scientific inquiry and discovery in Europe in the late 1600s. It continued through the 1700s and came to be called the Age of Enlightenment. The advances in many fields of knowledge included those in mapmaking.

New and more accurate maps became essential. The maps were needed because British, Spanish, French, and Dutch rulers began to seek the wealth of distant countries, such as China and India. From the 1500s through the 1700s, exploration and commerce were the driving forces behind the progress in **cartography**, the art of making maps.

Successful exploration depended not only upon better design and construction of sailing ships, but on greater accuracy in the maps used to navigate them. Maps were of great importance in reaching distant parts of the world as safely and swiftly as possible. Also, explorers could return to a newly discovered place of wealth, such as an island or an entire country, only if the area was mapped.

Many explorers were amateur mapmakers. In their notes, they described and estimated the size, shape, and distances between natural features they saw, such as inlets, bays, rivers, lakes, and mountains. They also drew rough maps of the area.

When they returned home, expert cartographers used their drawings, notes, and personal observations to create more detailed, professional maps.

Pirate Treasure Maps

Most maps were made to help sailors find islands in the oceans or help land travelers locate mountains or cities. However, some maps were drawn to locate hidden or buried treasure. Pirates often had to hide their loot from authorities or from other pirates, then come back for it later. A map helped them find their treasure.

The glory days of pirating were the 1500s and 1600s, mainly in the Caribbean. Ships bound for England, Spain, and other European countries were loaded with gold, silver, and jewels from Mexico and Central and South America. En route to their home ports, many of these treasure-laden ships sank in storms, and their precious cargo was lost at sea. Maps began circulating as to where such sunken ships could be found.

Many other treasure ships were robbed by pirates who then buried chests full of gold and silver in coastal caves or on remote islands. Often, maps were drawn so that the treasure could be located again. But, unfortunately for some pirates, many were hanged for their crimes before they could return for their treasure.

Captain Kidd's Treasure

Treasure-seekers today still follow so-called treasure maps hoping to find lost pirate loot. One of the most famous is a map of Oak Island off the coast of Nova Scotia. Since 1700, generations of treasure-hunters have been searching there for a pit believed to contain the buried treasure of Captain William Kidd, who became known as the most notorious pirate of them all.

This engraving shows part of the map French explorer Samuel de Champlain made of the northeast section of North America.

Chapter Four

Mapping New Lands

When colonists from Europe came to North America in the 1500s to 1700s, the need to explore and map the vast new territory became urgent. In the early 1500s, Spanish explorers surveyed and mapped the land in the south and southwest regions. Many years later, the French explorer Samuel de Champlain mapped the wilderness area from present-day Maryland to the St. Lawrence River and parts of the Atlantic coast.

Among the first Europeans to survey

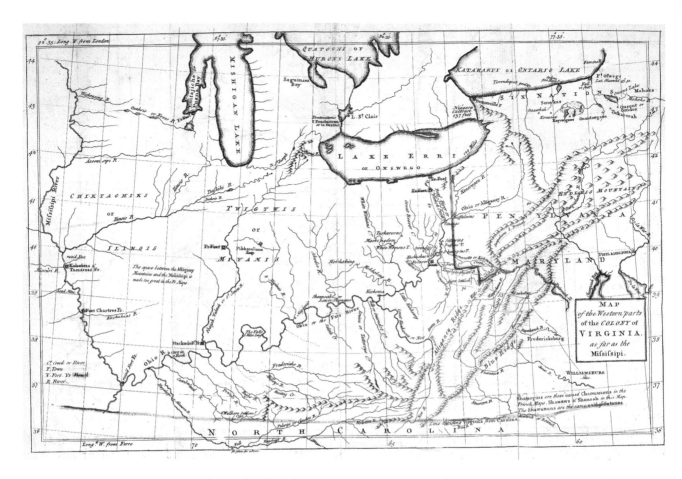

This map shows the Ohio country based on a map by George Washington.

colonial North America were Joshua Fry and Peter Jefferson. They produced a map of the region from Virginia to the Great Lakes in 1751. Four years later, John Mitchell, a Virginia colonist, published his Map of the British and French Dominions.

Maps were essential to both the British and the American armies in the Revolutionary War (1775–1783). George Washington had battle maps drawn to use to plan his military campaigns. After the war, John Mitchell's map was used to mark the boundaries of the new United States of America.

Thomas Jefferson, the third president of the United States, created the U.S. Public Land System that sent **surveyors** to map townships, roads, waterways, and mountain ranges. He also established a Survey of the Atlantic Coast in 1807 to provide for the safety of ships, passengers, and cargoes. Today, that agency is known as the National Ocean Service. Early maps also showed where Indian peoples were located in the United States and Canada.

Lewis and Clark Expedition

When the Louisiana Territory was purchased from France in 1803, this acquisition more than doubled the size of the United States. The purchase enlarged the new nation by 828,000 square miles (2.1 million square kilometers). The following year, President Thomas Jefferson authorized the largest mapping expedition in the nation's history.

Jefferson sent two experienced surveyors, Captain Meriwether Lewis and William Clark, to lead an exploration from St. Louis, Missouri, to the Pacific Ocean. Their journey began in 1804 and included a search for what was called the Northwest Passage, a hoped-for river route linking east and west. The two men surveyed the vast territory west of the Mississippi River all the way to the Pacific Ocean.

Traveling by land, lake, and river for two years, Lewis and Clark kept detailed notes of everything they saw. They were helped by a Shoshone Indian woman named Sacagawea whose French husband acted as an interpreter for the expedition. She

Lewis and Clark's expedition—called the Corps of Discovery— helped map the American West.

became their guide, and local Indians who drew maps for them on animal hides or on the ground.

Lewis and Clark's notes of the physical terrain and the area's plants and animals, as well as the longitude and latitude of the places they discovered, were then put on a master map. It was recorded on birch paper to prevent damage by moisture, including rain. Clark was the expedition's mapmaker, and in 1813 and 1814 he provided the information from which Samuel Louis prepared the final map, the first detailed map of the American West.

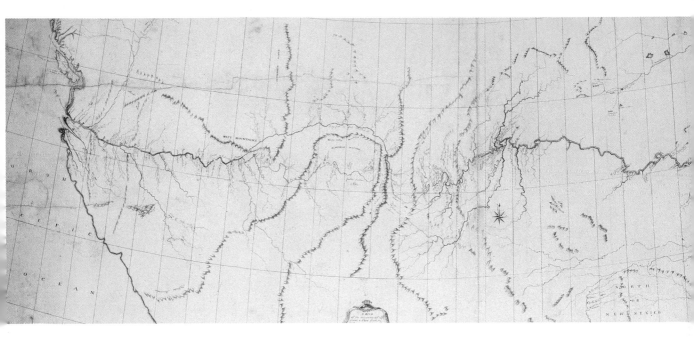

The Lewis and Clark map did not show a Northwest Passage from east to west in the United States because none existed. But the explorers discovered five passes through the Rocky Mountains into the Pacific Northwest's Oregon Territory. Their map became one of the most important ever drawn in North America. It was of great use in the westward expansion of the United States. Settlers wanted maps that could tell them about the land they were planning to farm. Prospectors wanted to know the location of minerals. Future mapmakers also drew upon the Lewis and Clark map of the West because of its accuracy.

This 1808 map shows the course that Lewis and Clark took on their journey.

Mapping Waterways

Not only did the land need to be mapped in pioneer times in North America, but the boundaries of its rivers and lakes

Daniel Boone

One of America's most famous frontiersmen, Daniel Boone, was also one of its busiest and most successful land surveyors. Between 1767 and 1773, he explored Kentucky and helped to colonize it.

John Wesley Powell faced many dangers as he explored the Colorado River.

needed to be recorded as well. An early explorer and surveyor of American rivers was John Wesley Powell, who braved the treacherous Colorado River in a small boat in 1869.

He and his guides rode the mighty river, running dangerous rapids, fearing hostile Indians, and never knowing whether the next rapids was a life-threatening waterfall. They followed the Colorado from its source in the high Rocky Mountains to the Gulf of California. Along the way, they became the first Americans to explore the Grand Canyon.

On a second expedition, Powell surveyed southern Utah and northern parts of Arizona and New Mexico to create maps that remained in use for nearly a hundred years. In 1881, Powell became director of the U.S. Geological Survey. By the time of his retirement in 1894, about one-fifth of the United States had been mapped to his demanding standards. The entire United States would not be totally mapped, however, until the 1980s.

The Mason–Dixon Line

One of North America's most important mapping expeditions came about because of an estate-boundary dispute between families in colonial times. They lived in the British colonies of Pennsylvania and Maryland in 1763. The disagreement led to what became the first professional boundary survey in America.

To settle the dispute, two Englishmen, astronomer Charles Mason and surveyor Jeremiah Dixon, were hired to survey the boundary between the two colonies. They worked on the project from 1763 to 1767 and faced many challenges, including severe winters and dangers from some hostile Indians. Helping them were workers who felled trees to clear sections of the wooded lands so that direct lines could be measured.

The line they drew was 233 miles (375 km) long at the thirty-ninth parallel of north latitude. (Most maps and globes show the nearby fortieth parallel, an imaginary horizontal line north of the equator.) Their work settled the boundary dispute between Pennsylvania and Maryland, and it became known as the Mason-Dixon Line. During the time of the American Civil War, it became the agreed-upon line dividing the free states of the North from the slave states of the South.

John Charles Frémont

Explorer and soldier John Charles Frémont began charting the Rocky Mountains in 1842. He and his guide, frontiersman Christopher "Kit" Carson, explored and mapped parts of Oregon, Nevada, and California.

People gather together to look at a map in this 1807 painting. During this time, people had more access to maps than ever before.

Chapter Five

Modern Mapmaking

The first half of the 1800s was a period of rapid progress in mapmaking. Maps that dealt with commerce and government were needed. Atlases and wall maps became available to both students of cartography and the general public. Detailed mapping of the world's coastlines also took place during this period, and topographic maps were made of both densely populated and sparsely settled parts of the globe.

Precision mapmaking instruments were invented in the 1700s and 1800s. They helped to produce more accurate maps than were possible with earlier astronomical methods. To locate places, astronomical methods simply noted the positions of the stars.

The telescope greatly increased the ease and accuracy of surveying. It uses lenses, mirrors, or both to gather light from a distant object and form a magnified optical image of it. Telescopes enabled navigators to more accurately identify coastal landmarks and other ships, which was especially important in wartime.

The Chronometer

A **chronometer** is an accurate timepiece such as a clock or watch used to determine longitude at sea or whenever an exact measurement of time is needed. A chronometer invented in 1735 was one of the great advances in the history of mapmaking. It also saved many lives, especially at sea.

For centuries, there was no accurate way to determine longitude (east/west location). But exact locations could only be found by knowing both longitude and latitude (or north/south location). Without accurate longitude, ships sank with their crews and passengers because the locations of rocky shores were miscalculated.

Longitude is measured in time. One degree of longitude corresponds to eight

This photograph shows a reproduction of the chronometer made by John Harrison.

minutes of a 24-hour day. A contest was held in England offering a large sum of money as a prize to anyone who could build an accurate chronometer. An English clockmaker, John Harrison, reasoned that the solution to the longitude mystery lay in building a clock that could maintain its accuracy at sea, since a ship's motion would throw a clock's pendulum out of order. He spent thirty years perfecting his chronometer—or longitude clock—in spite of the skepticism and opposition of many leading astronomers and British bureaucrats. However, it was finally accepted and, in 1762, John Harrison won the prize.

Maps Today

There are many different types of maps in use today. Topographical maps show features of the Earth's land surface and **road maps** show locations and distances between places. For oceans and other bodies of water, there are **nautical charts** that show coastal and marine areas. And **hydrographic charts** specify ocean depths and directions and intensities of oceanic currents. **Aeronautical charts** detail Earth's surface features and air routes. **Weather maps** show weather patterns.

In recent times, scientific and technological advances have revolutionized mapmaking. For example, **aerial photography** makes it possible to survey remote or inaccessible areas for more accurate topographic mapping. Despite extensive land surveying, most of the world remained largely unmapped until the advent of aerial photography in World War I (1914–1918). This resulted in the creation of world aeronautical charts with

Weather Maps

The first weather map was created in 1685 by Edmond Halley, an English astronomer and mathematician. It showed the **trade winds**, the system of winds that helped speed sailing ships. Although he created the first weather map, Halley is better known for the comet that bears his name. In 1682, Halley saw a great comet in the sky, calculated its path, and determined the comet—later called Halley's Comet—would reappear every 76 years.

general information for reconnaissance and other war purposes. However, an International Map of the World, begun in 1891, remains to be completed. It would be the most accurate and up-to-date map of national boundaries and resources, but some nations resist cooperating on the project for reasons of national security.

Surveying information obtained from **satellites** makes topographic mapmaking more accurate. Vast new knowledge for mapmaking comes from photographs taken by cameras on satellites that orbit in space. Most of the images come from

Mapping by Satellite

Information for modern mapmaking can be obtained from different types of cameras mounted on satellites that can photograph the Earth. Some work like ordinary cameras, taking pictures using the light of the Sun reflected off the Earth's surface. Others bounce microwave radar beams off the Earth's surface and use the reflected beams to create an image of the land. A third type creates images by recording the different amounts of infrared radiation given off by water, rocks, and vegetation.

Landsat satellites first launched by the United States in 1972 and new ones that are sent into orbit periodically.

In 1984, France launched the System Probatoire d'Observation de la Terre (SPOT) satellite. This satellite uses high surveying technology to produce very detailed data for maps of the world. Combinations of SPOT and Landsat data have been valuable in mapmaking.

Remote sensing imagery is another tool of modern mapping. This process obtains information about land, water, or an object such as a volcano without any physical contact with the subject. In mapping today, remote sensing refers to collecting data by infrared radiation, microwave, or other instruments

This map of the United States was created using many different images taken by the Landsat satellites.

carried aboard an aircraft or satellite. It is used to survey, map, and monitor the resources and environment of Earth and other planets. For example, remote sensors on weather satellites can track the movement of clouds and record temperature changes in the atmosphere.

How Maps Are Made

The five basic steps of modern mapmaking are observation and measurement of actual sites, database development, planning and graphic design, production and reproduction, and revision. For observation and measurement, surveyors determine boundaries and topographical features by measuring distances, angles, and heights at specific locations. Invention of the airplane in the early 1900s enabled mapmakers to survey by air. Today, satellites and spacecraft equipped with cameras and other data-gathering devices use aerial cartography at great distances from Earth.

Mapping information is acquired by observation and measurement, then stored electronically in computer records, called a database. In the United States, some of the largest databases of geographic information are maintained by the U.S. National Imagery and Mapping Agency, the U.S. Geological Survey, and the U.S. Bureau of the Census. Much of the map data is available free on CD-ROM disks for government, business, or home use.

Knowing what a map will be used for helps mapmakers decide its content and design. It also enables them to determine

The Geographic Information System

Another modern mapmaking tool is the Geographic Information System (GIS). It consists of computers, computer programs, and vast amounts of information stored as computer code. This includes measurements or photographs taken from land, sea, or space that are used to produce many different maps.

46

the best projection and **scale** for the map, as well as which features to include. Most often, a cartographer works with a graphic artist to design a map.

Regarding production and reproduction, most maps today are made by mechanical methods including computer printing. Some specialized maps are still drawn by hand. Computer map-printing tools include geographic information systems, mapping programs, and computer-aided design programs.

Many maps need periodic revision, especially after wars that result in national boundary changes. Also, populations of cities can change in census updates, the shapes of coastlines change from evolutionary forces, and areas of forest change when trees are felled for commercial or other reasons. Databases need to be frequently updated and maps must be revised to show these changes. Aerial photography often provides the new data for revisions.

A cartographer creates a map. The intended use for the map will influence how she designs it.

Maps of the Future

Today's high-technology maps enable scientists to use computerized maps to do many things, such as predicting earthquakes. Commercial and military airplanes fly more safely because of precise flight patterns mapped by computers and orbiting satellites. Maps drawn from computerized databases are made for a wide range of purposes, such as determining the environmental impact of a proposed construction project.

One of the most exciting and revolutionary developments in mapmaking today is the Global Positioning System (GPS). It is the only system today able to show an exact position on the Earth at any time and in any weather. The first GPS satellite was launched in 1978. Today there are twenty-four GPS satellites orbiting above the Earth, each transmitting signals from which those on the ground with a GPS receiver can determine location with great precision.

A GPS satellite orbits the Earth and helps people find their exact location on its surface.

But a GPS receiver isn't necessary to find virtually any place on Earth. All it takes these days is a personal computer. Using trip planning software or by searching the Internet, it is possible to find information on how to get just about anywhere, whether it is a block away from home or school or a world away.

It has long been said that a picture is worth a thousand words. So too, is a map. New maps drawn with modern technology, such as satellites and computers, convey more at a glance than any written document possibly could. They are vitally important aids in helping plan the future of the world in the new **millennium** and beyond.

The Internet allows people to get maps quickly and easily.

Timeline

2300 B.C.	Oldest-known map is drawn in Babylonia (now Iraq).
1000 B.C.	Polynesians explore the Pacific Ocean. Egyptians make maps.
550 B.C.	Greek geographer Anaximander creates a type of globe.
470 B.C.	Hanno of Carthage sails to West Africa.
240 B.C.	Greek mathematician Eratosthenes estimates circumference of the Earth.
115 B.C.	The Silk Road opens trade between China and the West.
A.D. 150	Greek astronomer Ptolemy draws a map of the world. Chinese astronomer Chang Heng develops grid system in mapmaking.
1155	Earliest printed map is drawn in China.
1200s	Portolan navigational charts are first drawn.
1253	Guillaume of Rubruqiuis explores Mongolia.
1400s	Prince Henry the Navigator explores the West Coast of Africa.
1436–1437	Johannes Gutenberg invents modern printing.
1487–1488	Bartolomeu Dias sails around the Cape of Good Hope at the tip of South Africa.
1492	Christopher Columbus arrives in North America on October 12. Martin Behaim creates first globe in western world.
1499	Amerigo Vespucci sails to West Indies.
1507	Martin Waldseemüller puts America on a map for the first time.
1521	Ferdinand Magellan's expedition completes the first voyage around the world.
1569	Gerardus Mercator publishes the Mercator projection map.

1570	Abraham Ortelius produces first modern world atlas.
1600s	Samuel de Champlain maps wilderness from Maryland to the St. Lawrence River.
1669	Giovanni Cassini begins work on the first topographical map of a nation, in France.
1685	Edmond Halley draws world's first weather map.
1762	John Harrison's chronometer helps determine accurate longitude.
1763–1767	Charles Mason and Jeremiah Dixon survey the boundary between two colonies.
1767–1773	Daniel Boone conducts land surveys of Kentucky.
1804–1806	Meriwether Lewis and William Clark explore and map Louisiana Territory from Missouri to the Pacific Ocean.
1807	Thomas Jefferson establishes Survey of the Atlantic Coast.
1842	John Charles Frémont charts the Rocky Mountains.
1869	John Wesley Powell surveys the Colorado River.
1891	An International Map of the World is begun.
1965	The Vinland Map is discovered.
1972	Landsat satellites are launched by United States to aid in mapmaking from space.
1978	Global Positioning System begins, providing satellite surveying from orbit in space.
1984	France's SPOT satellite is launched to provide detailed surveying of Earth.

Glossary

aerial photography—taking photos of the ground from airplanes

aeronautical chart—a chart that details the Earth's surface features and air routes

atlas—a book of maps

boundary—a line that marks the limit of one place, such as a state or country, and another

cartographer—a person who draws, plans, and studies maps

cartography—the making and studying of maps

chronometer—a clock that accurately measures time at sea. It is used to calculate a ship's longitude.

circumference—the distance around the rim or perimeter of a circle

compass—an instrument for determining direction with a magnetic needle showing where north is

current—a stream of water or air

equator—the imaginary line circling the Earth at latitude zero degrees. The starting point for measuring north and south on a map or globe.

explorer—a person who investigates unknown regions

globe—a sphere on which a map of the Earth or sky is drawn

grid—a system in which two sets of parallel lines that cross each other at right angles to form squares. It used for finding places on a map.

horizontal— parallel to the ground

hydrographic chart—a chart showing ocean depths and directions and intensities of oceanic currents

latitude—how far a place is to the north or south of the equator

longitude—how far a place is to the east or west of the prime meridian

map—a drawing, usually on a flat surface, of part or all of the surface of the Earth or sky

meridian—a line of longitude running north and south on a globe

millennium—a time period of one thousand years or ten centuries

nautical chart—a chart that shows coastal and marine areas

navigation—plotting a course from one place to another, whether on land, sea, or in the air

parallel—lines going in the same direction and the same distance apart

perpendicular—vertical or upright lines

portolan chart—a medieval chart that helped sailors reach their destinations at sea

prime meridian—an imaginary line that runs through Greenwich, England, marking the line of zero degrees longitude

projection—a method of showing the curved surface of the Earth on a flat map

road map—a map that shows the locations and distances between places

satellite—a human-made object launched from and orbiting Earth

scale—the sizes and distances between places on a map, compared to their actual sizes and distances

sea chart—a simple map that helps sailors locate places such as mainland coasts or islands

surveyor—a person who measures land

theologian—a person who studies religion

topographical map—a map showing features of the Earth's surface, such as hills or mountains

trade winds—winds that blow nearly constantly from the east in the tropics and subtropics

vertical—upright or straight up and down

weather map—a map that shows weather patterns

To Find Out More

Books

Blandford, Percy W. *The New Explorer's Guide to Maps and Compasses*. Blue Ridge Summit, PA: Tab Books, 1992.

Brewer, Paul. *The Golden Age of Exploration*. Vol. 2, *Explorers and Exploration*. Danbury, CT: Grolier, 1998.

Broekel, Ray. *Maps and Globes*. Chicago: Children's Press, 1983.

Carey, Helen H. *How to Use Maps and Globes*. New York: Franklin Watts, 1983.

Ganeri, Anita. *The Story of Maps and Navigation*. New York: Oxford University Press, 1997.

Graham, Alma. *Discovering Maps: A Young Person's World Atlas.* Maplewood, NJ: Hammond, 1981.

Harris, Nathaniel. *The Earliest Explorers.* Vol. 1, *Explorers and Exploration.* Danbury, CT: Grolier, 1998.

Johnson, Sylvia A. *Mapping the World.* New York: Atheneum, 1999.

Pratt, Paula Bryant. *Maps: Plotting Places on the Globe.* San Diego, CA: Lucent Books, 1995.

Stefoff, Rebecca. *Women of the World: Women Travelers and Explorers.* New York: Oxford University Press, 1992.

Organizations and Online Sites

American Revolution and Its Era
http://memory.loc.gov/ammem/gmdhtml/armhtml/armhome.html
This online site created by the Library of Congress displays maps and charts of North America and the West Indies from 1750 to 1789.

Ancient History: Maps
http://ancienthistory.about.com
This online site provides a wealth of information on maps and geography of the ancient world.

The National Atlas of the United States

http://www.nationalatlas.gov/

This online site is a companion to the print version of the National Atlas of the United States published by the U.S. Geological Survey and offers interactive maps on special topics online.

Orsher Map Library
University of Southern Maine
Box 9301
Portland, ME 04104

http://www.usm.maine.edu/~maps/

The Orsher Map Library at the University of Southern Maine contains a wide range of online exhibits about maps of the past and present.

A Note on Sources

I've always loved studying maps. When I was a boy growing up during World War II, I used to draw my own smaller-scale versions of full-page maps in the newspapers. Each day, they showed where the war was being fought in Europe, the Pacific, or Africa. I learned a great deal about world geography that way and developed a lifelong fascination with maps. I papered my college dormitory room with National Geographic maps, covering the ceiling as well as the walls.

When I research to write a book, I try to combine library research with contacting experts on the subject. In researching maps in history I had to rely primarily on libraries. I had the help of research librarians at four nearby libraries in Chicago, Evanston, Wilmette, and Glenview, Illinois. They recommended both adult and juvenile books on map history and I began by reading those for young readers, then graduated to the adult books. For young readers, I found the most helpful basic books on map history to be Nathaniel Harris's *The Earliest Explorers*, Paul Brewer's *The Golden Age of Exploration*, Alma Graham's *Discovering Maps*, and Ray Broekel's *Maps and Globes*. The most helpful adult books on map history were Norman Thrower's *Maps and Civilization* and David Woodward's *The History of Cartography*.

I also sit at my computer and go online to surf the World Wide Web for sites to help me research a subject. For researching the history of maps, the online sites I list in the To Find Out More section were especially helpful.

I always find researching a subject to be fascinating because it never fails that I learn more than I ever thought I would. It's really fun to share with readers little-known, often exciting, and sometimes funny things I find, such as those I include in this book about the adventures and dangers both men and women encountered on their mapmaking expeditions.

—*Walter Oleksy*

Index

Numbers in *italics* indicate illustrations.

About the Author

Walter Oleksy has been a freelance writer of books, mostly for young readers, for more than twenty-five years. He came to that occupation after several years as a newspaper reporter for *The Chicago Tribune* and as editor of three feature and travel magazines. A native of Chicago, he received a bachelor of arts degree in journalism from Michigan State University, then was editor of a U.S. Army newspaper for two years before starting his writing career.

He lives in a Chicago suburb with his best friend Max, a mix of Labrador retriever and German shepherd. They take frequent walks in the nearby woods and swim in Lake Michigan.

His most recent book for Children's Press is *The Philippines*. His other books for young readers include *Hispanic-American Scientists* and *American Military Leaders of World War II*.